W9-DEW-610

Wilanów

MUZEUM PAŁAC
W WILANOWIE

Wilanów

photographs
Paweł Jaroszewski

introduction
Paweł Jaskanis

Nobilis

Wilanów

Paweł Jaskanis

The Museum of the Palace in Wilanów is the guardian of monuments and memorial sites associated with King John III Sobieski (1629–1696). In the national tradition, the *genius loci* of Wilanów evokes the loftiest patriotic feelings and the formation of civic virtues at the service to the Republic *pro publico bono* (for the common good). The memorabilia of the Sobieski family would have not survived but for the special efforts of Stanisław Kostka Potocki (1755–1821), who started collecting artefacts associated with John III in the empty palace. In 1799 Potocki founded one of the first Polish museums in Wilanów, and then – on 5 August 1805, made it available to the general public. His grandson, August Potocki (1803–1867), continued his important work.

In the times of the Partitions of Poland and the country's lost independence, the institution established in Wilanów, along with other private museums, substituted non-existent state museums. Education through the nation's history and world art was extremely important at that time and today is also one of the fundamental elements of the museum's activity. Works of European and Asian art forming the core of Potocki's collection, offer an opportunity for a systemic lesson on history and art.

The origins of the residence date back to the mid-17th c., when the construction of a palace to the design of Giovanni Batista Gisleni was commissioned by Bogusław Leszczyński in the village of Milanów. On 23 April 1677 King John III purchased Milanów, where the "walls were built 3 ells above ground level". Probably at that time the estate was given a new name: Willanów (from the Italian term: *villa nuova*). Around ca. 1680 a brick manorhouse, with side annexes, not particularly impressive, was built on these foundations. In the years 1681 – 1696 a palace was built on the site in two stages to Agostino Locci's design and under his supervision. A team working at the palace consisted of Polish, Italian and French craftsmen and artists. The most renowned were the sculptor Stefan Szwaner, and the painters Claude Callot, Jerzy Eleuter Szymonowicz-Siemiginowski, Jan Reisner, Michelangelo Palloni and Martin Altomonte.

The next owner of the Wilanów estate, Elżbieta Sieniawska (1666–1729), developed the palace, adding two wings to Giovanni Spazzia's design in the 1720s. The work was initiated by Józef Fontana, and completed by Jan Zygmunt Deybel in the period during which the palace was leased to King August II the Strong (1670–1733). Outstanding sculptors, including Gianfrancesco Fumo and Jan Jerzy Plersch and the painter Giuseppe Rossi worked on that project. A large group of artists under the painter Johann Samuel Mock, an outstanding cabinet-maker and polisher Martin Schnell worked for the Vettin ruler. Not much is known about the patronage of the subsequent owners of the palace, the Czartoryskis. A bath pavilion was

01
A sundial on the palace façade dates from the 1680s. It is in the form of a spread textile fabric with Chronos above, being a Baroque allegory of time. The clock shows hours and days as a planetary cycle of cosmic changes which rule the world and human life.

02, 04
A bird's eye view of the Palace in Wilanów.

Wilanów

designed by Szymon Bogumił Zug, who also designed the Kitchen Outhouse and the Guardhouse nearby, commissioned by Elżbieta Lubomirska, née Czartoryska (1736–1816) and built at the southern wing. Ca. 1900, an upper floor was added to the pavilion. In the mid-19th c. Franciszek Maria Lanci built a Neo-Renaissance section to house new exhibition rooms and residential apartments on the upper floor.

After the death of Aleksandra Potocka (1818–1892), the museum and the landed estate were passed to Ksawery Branicki (1864–1926), who was a wealthy man, which was supposed to guarantee the proper care of historic buildings of Wilanów, its art collections, library and archives and the public function of the complex. Based on Adam Branicki's decision (1892 –1947) in 1932 the library was given to the President of the Republic of Poland in perpetual deposit. Most of the books in the collection survived the war as a part of the National Library in Warsaw. In the period of WWII, the residence was several times plundered by authorities of the 3rd Reich, occupying armies, German and Hungarian, and suffered damage. Most of the works of art were returned to Poland as early as 1945. Some artefacts which had been stolen by the Nazis were seized by the Red Army, so some of them returned no earlier than the 1950s. In 1945 the palace and the park complex was taken over by the state as part of the National Museum in Warsaw. After an extensive renovation project, completed in 1962, the palace was re-opened to the public.

The rich Baroque decor and furnishings, as well as the original form of the Potocki museum is not fully known to us. Fascinating research work continues in the hope that new facts and findings will be revealed to enrich the egalitarian programme of a modern museum.

The Wilanów Palace is one of the most precious jewels of the country's historic architecture, being the least damaged royal residence, and still retains its authentic spatial layout and the richness of its original decor. It is a unique phenomenon in Poland, considering the geopolitical situation of the country and numerous war cataclysms.

A complex of 32 historic buildings and two parks, in Wilanów and Morysin, separated by the old Vistula river bed, cover an area of nearly 90 ha, though this is only a part of the landscaping and economic complex of the former residence which once included the palaces and parks in Natolin, Gucin and Ursynów (formerly Roskosz). In 1994 the President of the Republic of Poland declared the area of the Wilanów and Morysin parks, together with elements of original park avenues running into the inner city of Warsaw, a Historic Memorial.

03
Wilanów Lake.

Wilanów

06
Main entrance to the Palace.

07
In the times of King John III, the Great Hallway was the most impressive, two-storey room of the palace on the axis of its main body (initially serving as the Dining Room), connecting royal apartments on both sides: on the right of the entrance – that of John III, while on the left that of Marie Casimire.
The present Neo-classical decor of walls lined with stuccowork imitation of marble was designed by Szymon Bogumił Zug in the 4th quarter of the 18th c. and was executed by Fryderyk Baumann. Plafond decorations and the frieze painted on canvas are works of H. Marconi and his son, Karol, dating from the mid-19th c.
The room is furnished with English chairs and armchairs from the late 18th c. and a French table with the onyx top on which stands an English lantern.

Wilanów

08

The King's Antechamber is an equivalent of the Queen's Antechamber situated on the other side of the Great Hallway. On the plafond, painted by J.E. Siemiginowski, there is an allegory of Winter. The frieze shows Bacchic scenes along with hunting and rural household occupations illustrating the quotations from Vergil's *Georgics*. The decorations of the mirror frames in the Regency style also allude to winter themes. Since the mid-18th c. the walls have been covered with patterned velvet in the style of Genoese textiles, dating from the years 1710-30.

09

The King's Bedroom is an equivalent of the Queen's Bedroom on the other side of the Dutch Study. The plafond was painted by J.E. Siemiginowski and depicts an allegory of Summer with a portrait of Marie Casimire as Aurora. The bed-moulding has decorations with putti on sea horses, intertwined dolphins and tondos depicting rural occupations in the summer, alluding to quotations from Vergil's *Georgics* on banderoles. The mirror frames in Regency style are adorned with attributes of the summer. The walls are lined with velvet from ca 1730 in the style of Genoa textiles. The interior is filled with 18th-century furniture. The canopy on a symbolically represented King's bed flanked by the panoplies consisting of Polish and Oriental military accessories.

Wilanów

 10

The Queen's Bedroom is one the most impressive Baroque rooms in the palace. The plafond is decorated with J.E. Siemiginowski's painting depicting the allegory of Spring. The bed-moulding is adorned with sphinxes and putti, while friezes depict rural spring occupations, illustrating the quotations from Vergil's *Georgics*. The framing of mirrors from the Regency period are adorned with motifs symbolising spring.

11

The Queen's Antechamber is the first room in the earliest, Baroque part of the palace which housed the King's and the Queen's rooms. It served as a vestibule, and its original decor has survived. The plafond is adorned with a painting on canvas by J.E. Siemiginowski (1681-1682) depicting the allegory of Autumn (allegories of other seasons may be seen in other royal rooms). Along the frieze are scenes depicting autumn occupations rural illustrating the quotations from Vergil's *Georgics* above. The mirror frames are in the Regency style and are also adorned with autumn motifs. Since the 1st half of the 18th c. the walls have been lined with patterned velvet dating from the years 1710-1730, in the style of Genoese textiles.

12
The Faience Study has preserved its 17th-century furnishing in its entirety. The walls are lined with Dutch tiles, adorned with gilt decorations which were very fashionable in Poland at that time. Main decorative motifs consist of vases framed with leaves and flowers, separated with strips with genre and Biblical scenes. The study is under a caisson cupola with stucco and painting decorations depicting three putti and a white eagle flying above with Sobieski's coat-of-arms.

13
Detail of caisson cupola decorations with stucco and painting composition with three putti.

Wilanów

14

The Middle Room is a
small chamber with a beam
ceiling typical of Old-Polish
nobility manor houses,
adorned with coats-of-
arms of John III and Marie
Casimire, crowns and
laurel wreaths. Portraits
of personages connected
with the court of August II
the Strong who resided in
Wilanów in the years 1730-
1733, August III and other
prominent figures who held
important state functions
are on display in this room.

Wilanów

Wilanów

15, 17
In the 19th c, the Vestibule was known as the "First Room". Its trompe d'oeil painting decoration from the 1st half of the 19th c. has survived. It was revealed under a layer of 19th-century pseudo-Chinese painting during conservation work which was carried out after WWII. The frescoes are works by Józef (Giuseppe) Rossi, the court painter of Elżbieta Sieniawska. The furniture chamber dates from the 1st half of the 18th c.

16
This room is a part of a complex of rooms for guests. It dates from the years 1850-1876, overlooking the garden on the first floor of the northern wing. It is furnished with furniture from the period of Warsaw Duchy.
A dummy is dressed in a livery coat of the Potocki family domestic service.

18 - 19
The Queen's Study known as the Mirror Study, has one of the most interesting Baroque decorations. The plafond painted on canvas depicts the Queen as Aurora, surrounded by her sons symbolising winds. The painting was done by Jan Reisner. The rich stuccowork decoration consists of the gilt framing of the plafond with garlands hanging down, as well as golden bouquets of flowers in the corners and winged sphinxes. The decoration is a work by the French sculptor and goldsmith J.Paris.

20
A copy of an antique sculpture in the Lower North Gallery.

21 - 22
The Etruscan Study was designed by Henryk and Leander Marconi after 1853 to serve as an exhibition room for the Wilanów collection of antique vases. The collection was initiated by Stanisław Kostka Potocki. When compared with other collections of that period, it was unique in that it was created not only by purchase but also as a result of archaeological excavations conducted by Potocki in late 1785 and 1786 in Nola near Naples. It originally consisted of 100 exhibits but in 1853 August Potocki extended it by purchasing vases which belonged to the Mikorski family along with their landed estate in Słubice near Gostynin. Floor tiles imitating mosaic were probably made in Berlin around 1850.

23

The collection of antiquities was established in 1875, and housed in a building to Leandro Marconi's design. It was commissioned by Aleksandra Potocka, who called it "the New Belvedere". It was aimed to house a collection of sculptures and fragments of Roman stone sarcophagi, mostly from the times of the Roman empire (2nd c. BC). Some of them had been collected by Izabela Lubomirska, the Marshal's spouse, and Stanisław Kostka Potocki. Architectural details, elements of sarcophaguses and reliefs were bricked in the western wall of the room. Statues and busts installed on pedestals and in recesses are either antique works dating from the 1st-2th c. AD, original works completed in later times, or modern copies dating from the 18th –19th c.

Wilanów

24
The King's Library – once a bi-partite room with an arcade, was formerly used by John III as a study in which he used to work and read. The original floor from three-colored marble tiles has survived, as the earliest floor preserved in the palace.

25
The Palace Chapel was built in the years 1852 –1861 at Aleksandra Potocka's (the wife of August Potocki) initiative in honour of John III Sobieski who died in Wilanów in 1696. The chapel was designed in 1852 by the Potocki architects: Henryk Marconi and Franciszek Maria Lanci working jointly. The altar with the tabernacle and the decorations of the walls, doors and windows are works of the Italian L. Carimini, while the statue taking the model from Rafael's Sistine Madonna was sculpted by the Italian V. Gaiassi.

26
(page 32-33)
The northern wing of the Palace.

Wilanów

Wilanów

27
In the western part of
the northern wing are
the Crimson Parlour and
the Bedroom with a Study.
In the 18th and the 19th c.
the rooms served as
dwelling rooms for the
owners of the palace –
the Sieniawski, Lubomirski
and Potocki families.
The original painting and
sculpture decor of the
plafonds from the period
in which this wing was built
(1726–29) has survived.
They are works by artists
who operated at the court
of Elżbieta Sieniawska –
the painter Józef (Giuseppe)
Rossi and stucco workers
Francesco Fumo and Pietro
I. Comparetti.
A particularly noteworthy
element of the Crimson
parlour is the plafond on
which the sky with flying
birds is painted, surrounded
with stuccowork exotic
birds and panoply motifs,
as well as banners with
the coats-of-arms of the
Sieniawski and Lubomirski
families. According to
source accounts the walls
of this room used to be
lined with Italian damask.
The room is adorned with
Silesian mirrors in the style
of Venetian mirrors from
the 18th c. Between the
mirrors hangs a portrait of
Natalia Sanguszko, née
Potocka, August Potocki's
sister (painted by Johann
Ender in 1829). The
parlour's furniture is in the
Empire style, of Russian
manufacture.

28
A German Empire desk, over which hangs *Allegory of History*, a painting by Nicolas Coypel.

29
The plafond decorations show allegorical figures representing faithfulness and justice combined with generosity, alluding to the virtues and merits of Marshal Stanisław Lubomirski.

30
The Bedroom and the Studiy which may be seen in the background are works of two eras. The painting decoration of the plafond and stuccoes on the bed-moulding date from the 18th c. while the eagles in the corners of the moulding, door finials and a set of Empire furniture date from the 19th c.

Wilanów

31
The Grand Crimson Room
was originally a suite
consisting of three rooms.
Around the mid-19th c.
it was remodelled to August
Potocki's order to house
a small museum exhibition
– mainly of foreign
paintings. The colour of
the walls – Pompeian rose,
as well as the painted
decoration of the plafond
with medallion portraits
by outstanding sculptors,
architects and painters of
the Renaissance, Baroque
and Classicism eras
– allude to typical 19th-
century museum interiors.
The walls are adorned with
European paintings from
the collection of Stanisław
Kostka Potocki and his
followers.

Wilanów

32
Detail of a caryatid
supporting the ceiling.

33
Detail of the decoration
of a bed-moulding
depicting playing putti,
which symbolise charm,
initiation and fertility.

34
Detail of a painting
composition on the ceiling
with a medallion portrait of
Hannibal Carracci by the
Berliner C. Hintze, 19th c.

Wilanów

35 - 36 - 37

The central part of the Grand Crimson Room gives access to he smaller Landscape Gallery.
Fine examples of landscape painting may be admired in its interior. Ancient plafond with imagery depicting Agriculture, Hunting and Shepherding and portraits of famous 17th- and 18th-century artists add to the beauty of thee room. The plafond is a work by the outstanding artist from Berlin, E. Bürger.

38
(next page)
The Grand Crimson Room.

Wilanów

39
Cast-iron staircase was executed in the mid-19th c. to Franciszek Maria Lanci's design.

40 - 41 - 42
The Collector's Study is an exhibition located in a few small rooms. The furnishing of this interior was inspired by a drawing by Anetka Potocka depicting Stanisław Kostka Potocki's study. A study was considered one of three places important for a gentlemen's education, next to a garden and a library. The garden enabled direct contact with nature, full of harmony and beauty, symbolising the ideal world. A library was filled with educational resources – manuscripts, old prints, drawings and engravings which documented past events, science and art disciplines of interest for a young gentlemen.

43
The Lower North Gallery connects both wings of the palace with the main body. In 1820 Stanisław Kostka Potocki decided the gallery to be used as a museum and for this purpose to wall it up from the side of the garden up to the mid-height of the gallery. Along with a room in the north wing these structures formed a Wilanów pinakotheke (collection of paintings), open to the general public. It was restored to its original appearance during post-war conservation work. The walls and the plafonds of the gallery are adorned with frescoes which were revealed from under the plaster. They were commissioned by King John III and painted by Michelangelo Palloni ca 1688. One of the most interesting exhibits in the Wilanów collection is a portrait of Stanisław Kostka Potocki on horseback, signed "J.L. David 1781", displayed in the room. Copies of antique sculptures – 18th- and 19th-century busts on gilt consoles are also on display.

44
The statue of John III Sobieski on horseback, shown as a vanquisher of the Turks, originally was installed in a recess between the columns in the Great Hallways, facing the main entrance to the palace. It was made in plaster ca 1693 by a royal sculptor, whose name remains unknown.

45 - 46

The Study in front of the Gallery (in the 17th c. two-partite, known as the "Backyard Study") led from the northern gallery to the apartment of Queen Marie Casimire and was richly adorned with stucco decoration on the ceiling and the walls lined with coloured velvet.

The present decor with the allegory of Painting on the plafond dates from the years 1850-1857. The Study is furnished in the style recalling its appearance in the mid-19th c. On the walls hang paintings which have survived from the original Stanisław Kostka Potocki's gallery.

47
(next page)
The southern wing of the Palace.

Wilanów

48

The White Room was designed by Jan Zygmunt Deybl. It was built in the years 1730–1733 for King August II, who used Wilanów on the basis of an agreement with the Czartoryski family. it is the most splendid room in all the palace. It seems larger than it actually is, due to the mirrors hung on the wall facing the window. On the axis of the room there are two fireplaces in which cast-iron plates with August II initials have survived. Over the fireplaces there are two galleries for the court musical ensemble which were revealed during post-war conservation works.

49 - 50
The bathroom is one
of the most impressive
and splendid rooms of
the bath pavilion, built
on Duchesse Lubomirska's
initiative in the years 1775
–1778 to Szymon Bogumił
Zug's design. Its walls are
adorned with white and
green stuccowork.
The marbled bathtub
is installed centrally in
a niche. An interesting
element of the interior is
a stuccowork canopy,
surmounted with an ostrich
panache. A sofa stands
under the canopy.

Wilanów

51
Chinese rooms are on the first floor of the southern wing. They were arranged by the Potockis in the 19th c. The ceiling is covered with decorations featuring dragons and masks while the walls are lied with wallpaper with Chinese motifs.

52
A view of the Palace
from north-east.

The Rose Garden in the
southern wing of the palace
was commissioned by August
and Aleksandra Potocki
and developed in the years
1855-1856 to the design
of the architect Bolesław
Paweł Podczaszyński.

Wilanów

Wilanów

54

A two-level, Italian Baroque garden forms the central part of the Wilanów garden, situated between the palace and the lake. The upper garden consists of a terrace decorated with geometrical patterns of parterres lawns and boxwood hedge with motifs of fleur-de-lys and palmettes, and with fountains. The lower Baroque garden is a little different from the upper garden. In addition to decorative parterres, the tall clipped bosquets form the main element of its composition.

55

A statuette by the fountain in the Neo-Renaissance Garden, known as the Rose Garden, features a boy with a swan. It was cast in Karol Minter's manufacture in Warsaw in the mid-19th c.

Wilanów

57
The orangery was built in the mid- 18th c. to Jan Zygmunt Deybl's design. In 1811 it was remodelled in the Neoclassical style with a portico from the side of the lake, designed by Chrystian Piotr Aigner.

Wilanów

58
Leda with a swan – a late-Baroque Silesian sculpture from the years 1729-1734.

59
Jove – a late-Baroque Silesian sculpture from the years 1729–1734.

60
(page 74–75)
The pump house is a pseudo-mediaeval building supplying water to garden fountains. It was built to Henryk Marconi's design in 1856, on the site where the Baroque Garden meets the English-style garden.

Wilanów

61

A richly polychromed structure with reconstructed fresco decorations by A. Dąbrowski and J. Stankiewicz, designed by Piotr Aigner in 1806 in accordance with Oriental trends in garden architecture which were fashionable at the time.

62

Hercules with a club and an apple from the Garden of Hesperides – a late-Baroque Silesian sculpture from the years 1729-1734.

63

(next page)
An English-style landcsape park was planned in the years 1799 – 1821. At that time Stanisław Kostka Potocki with his wife Aleksandra decided to extend the park area to the north and to plan it in the style of English landscape parks which were fashionable at that time. The garden was developed step by step, as it required the changes in the land sculpture, such as the building of a weir and an island, the planting of trees and shrubs, the construction of structures in the style of romanticism. Wilanow Lake with its water reservoirs and picturesque banks have always formed a very important element of the northern part of the park and still do. At one time the park was considered one of the largest water gardens in Europe.

Nobilis

Wydawnictwo „Nobilis" Krzysztof Sobieraj

ul. Dominikańska 33
02-738 Warszawa
tel./fax: (22) 853-12-61, e-mail: nobilis_1@wp.pl

Photographs
Paweł Jaroszewski

Introduction
Paweł Jaskanis

Consultation
Wiesław Malawski

Description of photographs
The Museum of the Palace in Wilanów

Design
PaArt

Translation
Małgorzata Walczak, Charles Warburton
Letterman

The publisher wishes to thank the Museum of the Palace in Wilanów for kind assistance due to which the publication of this book was made possible.

The author of photographs thanks the staff of the Museum of the Palace in Wilanów for their kind assistance in his work.

Printing
Łódzka Drukarnia Dziełowa
90-215 Łódź, ul. Rewolucji 1905 r. nr.45

ISBN
978-83-60297-20-9